Editor
Nancy Hoffman

Managing Editor
Karen J. Goldfluss, M.S. Ed.

Cover Artist
Brenda DiAntonis

Art Manager
Kevin Barnes

Art Director
CJae Froshay

Imaging
James Edward Grace
Rosa C. See

Publisher
Mary D. Smith, M.S. Ed.

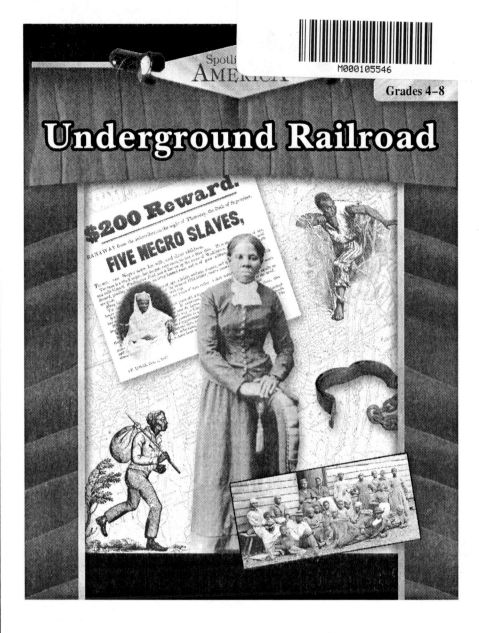

Grades 4–8

Underground Railroad

Author

Robert W. Smith

Teacher Created Resources, Inc.
6421 Industry Way
Westminster, CA 92683
www.teachercreated.com

ISBN: 978-1-4206-3215-6

©2005 Teacher Created Resources, Inc.
Reprinted, 2011
Made in U.S.A.

Table of Contents

Introduction

The *Spotlight on America* series is designed to introduce significant events in American history to students in the fourth through eighth grades. Reading in the content area is enriched with a balanced variety of activities in written language, literature, social studies, oral expression, and science. The series is designed to make history literally come alive in your classroom and take root in the minds of your students.

The Underground Railroad transformed slaves' desire for freedom and Northern abolitionists' deep commitment to personal liberty into a realistic effort to break the chains of slavery and to end this system in the United States. Men and women were so dedicated to the belief in liberty and the ideals of this nation that they risked their lives and fortunes to rescue slaves who were trying to escape from their masters and slavery.

The heroes of this movement were Quaker farmers, freed blacks, ministers of several faiths, fugitive slaves, women's rights advocates, Oberlin college students, Massachusetts intellectuals, and radical newspaper publishers. Together they worked to get slaves to free states and Canada and to change the nation's attitude towards slavery.

The strict enforcement of the new Fugitive Slave Law of 1850 led to relentless efforts to return slaves to their owners and punish the conductors of the Underground Railroad. Some slaves were returned to slavery forever. Some members of the Underground Railroad were fined, jailed, attacked by mobs, and lost everything they owned. They simply would not quit, however. The Civil War with its ultimate Union victory was in part caused by the activities of the Underground Railroad, which eventually freed all slaves.

The reading selections and comprehension questions in this book introduce the Underground Railroad. They set the stage for activities in other subject areas. The writing and oral language activities are designed to help students sense the drama and danger, fear and peril which accompanied every escape. Students should acquire an understanding of the urgency of events and the social, cultural, and economic background during this time period. The literature activities are intended to literally bring students into the lives of people as diverse as Thomas Garrett, William Still, Eliza Harris, Ellen and William Craft, Harriet Tubman, and the family of Levi Coffin. The culminating activities aim to acquaint students with the life and times of people involved in the pursuit of liberty.

Enjoy using this book with your students. Look for other books in this series.

Teacher Lesson Plans for Reading Comprehension

Beginning of the Underground Railroad

Objective: Students will demonstrate fluency and comprehension in reading historically based text.

Materials: copies of Beginning of the Underground Railroad (pages 7–9); copies of Beginning of the Underground Railroad Quiz (page 21); additional reading selections from books, encyclopedias, and Internet sources for enrichment

Procedure

1. Reproduce and distribute Beginning of the Underground Railroad. Review pre-reading skills by briefly reviewing the text and encouraging students to underline, make notes in the margins, list questions, and highlight unfamiliar words as they read.

2. Have students read the article independently, in small groups, or together as a class.

3. As a class, discuss the following questions or others of your choosing.
   - Why do you think that some people became abolitionists?
   - Why did some slaves run away from their owners and others refuse to leave?
   - What would you have done if you were a slave—try to escape or stay a slave?
   - What hardships and suffering did fugitive slaves endure?

Assessment: Have students complete the Beginning of the Underground Railroad Quiz. Correct the quiz together.

Underground Railroad Terms

Objectives: Students will demonstrate fluency and comprehension in reading historically based text and will apply their language arts skills in vocabulary enrichment.

Materials: copies of Underground Railroad Terms (page 10) and copies of Underground Railroad Terms Quiz (page 22)

Procedure

1. Reproduce and distribute Underground Railroad Terms. Review pre-reading skills by briefly reviewing the text and encouraging students to underline, make notes in the margins, list questions, and highlight unfamiliar words as they read.

2. Have students read the article independently, in small groups, or together as a class.

3. As a class, review the Underground Railroad terms. Discuss the following questions or others of your choosing.
   - Why did pilots have to talk slaves into escaping?
   - Why did people become pilots, conductors, ticket agents, and stationmasters on the Underground Railroad?
   - Why did slaves try to escape to Canada?
   - Would you have helped in the Underground Railroad? What would you have done?

Assessment: Have students complete the Underground Railroad Terms Quiz. Correct the quiz together.

Teacher Lesson Plans for Reading Comprehension *(cont.)*

Leaders of the Underground Railroad

Objective: Students will demonstrate fluency and comprehension in reading historically based text.

Materials: copies of Leaders of the Underground Railroad (pages 11–14); copies of Leaders of the Underground Railroad Quiz (page 23); additional reading selections from books, encyclopedias, and Internet sources for enrichment

Procedure

1. Reproduce and distribute Leaders of the Underground Railroad. Review pre-reading skills by briefly reviewing the text and encouraging students to underline, make notes in the margins, list questions, and highlight unfamiliar words as they read.

2. Have students read the article independently, in small groups, or together as a class.

3. As a class, discuss the following questions or others of your choosing.
   - Who was the most interesting leader of the Underground Railroad? Why?
   - Which leader did you admire the most? Why?
   - Why did these leaders take the chances they did?

Assessment: Have students complete the Leaders of the Underground Railroad Quiz. Correct the quiz together.

Passengers on the Underground Railroad

Objective: Students will demonstrate fluency and comprehension in reading historically based text.

Materials: copies of Passengers on the Underground Railroad (pages 15–18); copies of Passengers on the Underground Railroad Quiz (page 24); additional reading selections from books, encyclopedias, and Internet sources for enrichment

Procedure

1. Reproduce and distribute Passengers on the Underground Railroad. Review pre-reading skills by briefly reviewing the text and encouraging students to underline, make notes in the margins, list questions, and highlight unfamiliar words as they read.

2. Have students read the article independently, in small groups, or together as a class.

3. As a class, discuss the following questions or others of your choosing.
   - Which escape took the most courage? Why?
   - Which fugitive slave did you most admire? Why?
   - What fears would a fugitive slave have to overcome?

Assessment: Have students complete the Passengers on the Underground Railroad Quiz. Correct the quiz together.

Teacher Lesson Plans for Reading Comprehension *(cont.)*

The End of the Line

Objective: Students will demonstrate fluency and comprehension in reading historically based text.

Materials: copies of The End of the Line (pages 19 and 20); copies of The End of the Line Quiz (page 25); additional reading selections from books, encyclopedias, and Internet sources for enrichment

Procedure

1. Reproduce and distribute The End of the Line. Review pre-reading skills by briefly reviewing the text and encouraging students to underline, make notes in the margins, list questions, and highlight unfamiliar words as they read.

2. Have students read the article independently, in small groups, or together as a class.

3. As a class, discuss the following questions or others of your choosing.

   • Was war the only way that slavery could have been abolished? Why or why not?

   • How did the Underground Railroad lead to the abolition of slavery?

   • Why did the army and government have to help freed slaves during the Civil War?

   • What would fugitive slaves and freed slaves have to learn?

Assessment: Have students complete The End of the Line Quiz. Correct the quiz together.

Reading Passages

Beginning of the Underground Railroad

A Railroad Without Trains

The *Underground Railroad* was not a railroad at all. It was a means of escape for fugitive slaves running away from their masters. The Underground Railroad had no trains and no tracks, but it guided thousands of fleeing slaves along an informal network of secret hiding places from the slave states to the northern United States and Canada. There was no official leader or organization. Sympathetic whites, members of some religious groups (especially the Quakers), freed blacks, and other slaves helped runaway slaves escape their pursuers.

Fugitives traveled north for hundreds of miles by hidden routes and sometimes in disguise through rugged forests, across icy rivers, through slave states, into the Northern states, and on to Canada. Freedom-seeking slaves were hidden in closets, caves, cellars, barns, secret rooms, stables, abandoned buildings, sheds, and under wagon loads of hay or vegetables. They were often hidden during the day and moved at night from one station to another. Secret codes, signs, and symbols—often displayed on quilts—helped these volunteer rescuers communicate with each other.

The Underground Railroad

The term *Underground Railroad* was first used about 1830 by a Southern slave catcher who remarked that the runaway slave seemed to vanish into an "underground railroad." Slaves had, of course, been attempting escape and sometimes succeeding in the 200 years before this, but the escapes were much more organized and effective from 1820 until the Civil War began in 1861.

The first organized effort by whites and blacks to help escaping slaves was probably formed around 1819 when a man named Vestal Coffin organized a series of hiding places and escape routes. For security reasons, no one ever knew the true extent of the organization or how many slaves were actually helped. Estimates run from 40,000 to 60,000 but the actual number may have been higher.

Beginning of the Underground Railroad *(cont.)*

Runaway Slaves

Slaves escaped from all areas of the South, but the most successful escapes occurred in the border states of Kentucky, Virginia, and Maryland, which were close to free states and where many blacks and whites worked together to assist fleeing slaves. Fugitive slaves traveled along a well-organized chain of "stations" in Illinois, Indiana, Western Pennsylvania, and New York to reach Canada, "the promised land."

Unguarded Borders

The long, unguarded Pennsylvania border was inviting to blacks trying to flee the slave states of Virginia and Maryland, especially from cities like Baltimore. It became increasingly difficult for escaping slaves to stay in the free Northern states—even New York and Massachusetts—after the passage of the tough Fugitive Slave Act in 1850.

Fugitive Slave Law

The Fugitive Slave Law required Northern citizens, law officers, judges, and other officials to return escaped slaves to their owners. It included a huge $1,000 fine and six-months jail time for people who refused to cooperate. Southern slave hunters often traveled through border states and free states, capturing not only escaped slaves but free blacks as well and then taking them South. This law caused widespread anger, increased participation in the Underground Railroad, and helped divide the North and South even further.

Southern Slavery

Black laborers had been imported to the colony of Jamestown shortly after its establishment. Slavery spread throughout all of the English colonies in America, but it became the backbone of the economy in the Southern colonies. The invention of the cotton gin in 1793 made slavery enormously profitable. Plantation owners raised huge crops of cotton, which were grown and harvested with slave labor. Cotton became the basis of the Southern economy and was a huge cash crop exported to the Northern states and Europe. Slaves were almost as numerous as whites in many Southern states. When the Civil War began in 1861, there were four million black slaves in the South and five million whites.

Northern Slavery

Settlers in the Northern colonies owned some black slaves who worked on their small farms. Often the slaves were household servants or helped craftsmen, mill owners, and other tradesmen who often taught these skills to their slaves. Many of these slaves eventually earned or were granted their freedom. By the end of the American Revolution, slavery had largely ended in the Northern states and soon became illegal in most Northern states. Slaves never made up a large part of the population in the North.

Beginning of the Underground Railroad *(cont.)*

Escaping Slavery

Slaves ran away for many reasons. The most common, of course, was the desire to live as free people. As slaves, they were subjected to harsh and endless labor with no pay and often to brutal physical punishments designed to keep them fearful and obedient. The death of an owner often meant that slave families would be broken up and sold. Sometimes a father would escape to freedom in the hope that he could later rescue his wife and children, an event that rarely happened because mothers and children were divided and often sold to owners in distant places.

The Runaways

Most runaways were young men who were more likely to survive the long journey to freedom. Fugitives had great difficulty finding food and traveling through unknown forests and across land they had never seen, guided only by the North Star and by the kindness of a sympathetic slave or white. A runaway slave usually had to travel by foot with only the clothes on his or her back to protect against bitter cold nights, soaking rains, and the blistering, hot sun.

Despite the hardships some women, children, entire families, and older slaves also braved terrible punishment and death rather than remain in slavery. Slaves were always at risk from local sheriffs, gangs of brutal slave catchers, local lynch mobs, and individuals who wanted the monetary reward for returning an escaped slave. A few runaways hid in Southern cities like Atlanta where they blended in with the local black population. Some formed armed, rough camps in the unsettled Southern forests or mountains where they were difficult to locate.

Slavery's Opponents

In the mid-1830s a number of ministers, writers, and public officials in the North began calling for the complete abolition, or end, of slavery. These abolitionists cited a "higher law" (from God), greater than the Constitution, in their struggle to end slavery. They became important leaders and supporters of the Underground Railroad because they quickly recognized that one way to break the power of the slaveholders was to assist runaway slaves. Helping the fugitives became a way opponents of slavery could immediately do something to end slavery, at least for a few black Americans.

The Quakers, a religious group opposed to slavery, were deeply involved in this enterprise. One Quaker named Levi Coffin (a cousin to Vestal Coffin) helped organize the Underground Railroad and personally participated in the escape of more than 2,500 fugitive slaves. The gradual effect of these antislavery efforts was to convince many Northerners that slavery was wrong.

 Reading Passages

Underground Railroad Terms

Pilots

Pilots were particularly courageous men and women who went South to encourage slaves to run away from their owners. Many of these were former slaves who had to remain in hiding and secretly meet with slaves they felt might want to run away. Some were whites who traveled openly in the South because of their color but who were subjected to jail, torture, or even hanging if they were caught.

Conductors

Conductors of the Underground Railroad did not take tickets. However, they were often the ticket to freedom for escaping slaves. Usually conductors guided slaves from one hiding place to another. They might hide the escapees in plain sight as personal servants or slaves. The conductor might disguise the escapees or hide them under a wagon load of hay or drive them at night to another secret location.

Stationmasters and Stations

The *stationmaster* of the Underground Railroad was an individual or family who provided a hiding place for fugitive slaves. These hiding places were called *stations* or *depots*. They might be as simple as a cave, a cellar, or a barn or as complicated as secret rooms, hidden closets, or even boxes. Stationmasters took great risks because many in the community disapproved of their efforts, and they faced serious legal problems if caught.

Passengers/Cargo

The *passengers* were the runaway slaves. Like passengers on a train, they could not choose the route they traveled and had to have faith in the goodwill of their conductors and stationmasters. On this railroad, the *cargo*, another name for passengers, had to be fed and clothed as well as transported. Sometimes they had to be treated for illnesses and injuries as well.

Terminals

The final destination for many freedom seekers was Canada. The *terminals* for the Underground Railroad were homes, shelters, and communities along the Canadian shore of Lake Erie and other places bordering the United States.

Other Terms

Smooth trips were successful escapes in which the fugitives made it North and consequently to freedom. If the *train ran off the track*, it meant that "the fugitives had been recaptured and returned to their owners." Abolitionists and other people who fiercely opposed slavery and who talked slaves into escaping were known as *ticket agents*. Those who helped escaped slaves once they were in free states were known as *brakemen*. The entire Underground Railroad network was often referred to by its initials, UGRR.

 Reading Passages

Leaders of the Underground Railroad

Harriet Tubman

The greatest conductor of the Underground Railroad was a runaway slave named Harriet Tubman, known to those she helped escape as "Moses." Born as one of 11 children in a slave family, she was mistreated and beaten by her master, who often rented her out to other people. She was once hit on the head so hard by an overseer that she suffered a kind of drowsiness the rest of her life if she was not active. Finding that two of her brothers and she were going to be sold to another owner, Harriet decided to escape even though her husband and brothers were reluctant to join her.

Harriet escaped from her owner in Maryland and got to Pennsylvania, a free state. She tried to return and rescue her husband, but he had already remarried and refused to flee. Gradually, Harriet established a route of Underground Railroad stations and made more than 20 trips into Southern states, rescuing her two brothers, many other members of her family, and over 300 other slaves. Slave owners posted rewards for her capture totaling over $40,000. Harriet carried a pistol on her rescue missions and threatened to shoot anyone who refused to cooperate once they were on the run.

Harriet became a famous antislavery speaker and activist and helped John Brown recruit some of his followers. During the Civil War, Harriet served as a spy, scout, and nurse for the Union army. After the war she set up her own home as a refuge for needy freed slaves.

Thomas Garrett

One of the greatest stationmasters of the Underground Railroad was Thomas Garrett, a Quaker from Delaware who helped shelter and transport more than 2,700 escaped slaves along secret escape routes. The state of Maryland once offered a reward of $10,000 (an immense sum of money at the time) for his capture. He joked that if they doubled the reward, he would capture himself.

In 1848 Garrett was arrested and fined $5,400 for helping fugitive slaves. He had to auction off all his possessions to pay the fine but refused to quit. Despite the severe punishments, Garrett declared that if anyone knew of a fugitive who needed help, he would be happy to provide a meal and a place to hide.

William Wells Brown

William Wells Brown was born a slave. He tried to escape with his mother, but they were caught. His mother was sold away to the deep South in New Orleans, and he never saw her again. Later, Brown escaped from his owner and reached the free state of Illinois, where he set up a ship business. He allowed slaves to escape on his ships, which carried many fugitives to free soil. Later in life, he became a writer and a self-taught doctor.

 Reading Passages

Leaders of the Underground Railroad *(cont.)*

John Fairfield

John Fairfield was born into a white, slaveholding Virginia family. For many years, Fairfield traveled through the Southern states posing as a slave trader but carefully seeking slaves who wanted to escape. Using his perfect cover as a slaver, he managed to bring hundreds of slaves to freedom in the North. He was especially adept at locating and rescuing the wives and children of men who had escaped to freedom. Fairfield was still trying to bring out fugitives when he was killed during a slave revolt in Tennessee in 1860.

Josiah Henson

Josiah Henson, a Maryland slave, was whipped with more than 100 lashes for trying to protect his mother from a vicious overseer. His ear was nailed to the whipping post and then cut off. Josiah's father was sold and never seen again. Josiah was beaten so badly by another overseer that he could never lift his arms above his head again. He finally ran away through the wilderness of Indiana and Ohio with his sick wife and his children. Facing starvation and threatened by hungry wolves, Henson and his family eventually made it to Canadian soil. He learned how to work and survive in Canada and taught other fugitives the lessons he had learned about growing crops and living as a free person.

Henson later walked more than 400 miles back to Kentucky to rescue the family of his friend, James Lightfoot. They were too fearful to flee so he ended up helping another group of 30 slaves who lived more than 50 miles away. These fugitives from several states banded together to escape, and he led them across the Ohio River through Indiana and on to Canada.

A year later, Henson returned to Kentucky for the Lightfoot family, who had finally decided they wished to escape. With slave catchers hot on their trail, Henson helped them organize their escape and led them to Canada. Later in life he became a minister. Henson was also the first fugitive slave to have an audience with Queen Victoria in England.

Richard Daly

Richard Daly was a trusted slave who lived in Kentucky near the Ohio River. He was married to a slave and had four children but chose not to escape and leave them. However, he helped more than 30 slaves escape by ferrying them across the Ohio River at night and then passing the runaways on to an agent of the Underground Railroad. When his wife died at the age of 20, Daly escaped with his children before they could be separated and sold away.

 Reading Passages

Leaders of the Underground Railroad *(cont.)*

John Parker

By all standards, John Parker was an exceptional man. He was a freed black who lived and owned a foundry in the antislavery community of Ripley, Ohio. One of 500 black conductors of the Underground Railroad, Parker spent many nights secretly rowing a boat across the wide expanse of the Ohio River looking for fugitives.

Many nights he ventured through the plantations of northern Kentucky looking for runaways to help. Once he went to rescue a couple, but they would not leave without their baby who was forced to sleep at the foot of their owner's bed as insurance against their escape. Parker slipped into the house, grabbed the baby, knocked a candle and a loaded pistol off a stand, and raced away with the baby and couple. He got them across the river and hidden before the owner could find them. Parker became a legend among fugitive slaves and an enemy to slave catchers.

William Still

William Still was the son of an escaped slave named Charity, who on her second attempt managed to run away from her Maryland owners with her two daughters. She joined her free husband in a backcountry area of New Jersey. As a young man, William went to work for the Anti-Slavery Society in Philadelphia and was soon involved in all of the efforts to help fugitives escape. He began to keep detailed accounts of the adventures and escapes of the people he helped, which were published after slavery ended.

Still helped move escapees along the network through Philadelphia to Boston, New York, and Canada. One of his "passengers" was his long-lost brother Peter, who his mother had been forced to leave when she escaped decades before. Still used a quirk in the law to free the slaves of a U.S. ambassador who had been brought to Philadelphia and desired freedom. In his later years, Still became a successful businessman who supported blacks in their struggle for equality.

Reverend John Rankin

The Reverend John Rankin was a true believer in the abolitionist cause. A determined and fiery Presbyterian minister, he tried to convince his Kentucky neighbors of the evils of slavery. When he moved to Ripley, Ohio, Rankin became a leader in the Underground Railroad. He and his wife helped move untold numbers of escaping slaves along the route to freedom. Working with many black and white supporters, they secretly moved runaways into safe locations.

Eliza Harris, who crossed the Ohio River with her child in her arms, was hidden by Rankin in his own home. In the year after her escape, Eliza returned hoping to find her remaining slave children. John Rankin helped her return to Kentucky and escape again, this time with her other five children.

 Reading Passages

Leaders of the Underground Railroad *(cont.)*

Jonathan Walker

In 1844 Jonathan Walker was a white shipbuilder who tried to help seven slaves escape to the Bahamas. They were caught, and the slaves were returned to their owners. Walker was taken to Florida, made to pay a heavy fine, put on public display so that people could throw rotten eggs at him, and branded on the hand with "SS" indicating a slave stealer. Walker went North where he was a popular speaker at abolitionist meetings and helped other slaves escape.

Levi and Catherine Coffin

Levi and Catherine Coffin, members of the Quaker faith which opposed slavery, ran the Underground Railroad's "Grand Central Station." As a young man, Levi began helping slaves escape in his community of New Garden, North Carolina. He made it a point to give food and clothing to runaways and help them find a place to hide and a route North. When he moved to Newport, Indiana, in 1826, his red brick home became a stopping place for over 100 runaways a year as they passed through on their way to Canada. He often hid fugitives in a space under the eaves of his house in an attic with a bed that covered their hiding place.

Levi and his wife Catherine often helped slaves travel through areas patrolled by slave catchers by disguising them. Males were often disguised as females, and many females were dressed as workingmen or clothed in simple Quaker garb. This clothing covered even the faces and hands of the escapees. Runaways were often hidden in the false bottoms of wagons and moved to other stations along the route to freedom.

Levi visited freed slaves in Canada and came back more determined than ever to raise money for freed blacks and assist those on the run. For more than 25 years, the Coffin home was a way station, hiding place, and refuge for more than 2,500 slaves on the run. Their organization of freed blacks, dedicated fellow Quakers, and determined antislavery advocates was a constant source of help to fugitive slaves. Coffin, his family, and his associates were often threatened by angry slave owners and gangs of slave catchers, but they stayed at their posts until the Civil War ended slavery.

Other Heroes

No one knows the names of all of the people who helped slaves escape along the Underground Railroad, and the stories of many of them are lost forever. One group of five families in southern Ohio helped hide more than 1,000 runaways. Dr. Nathan Thomas of Michigan helped as many as 1,500 slaves reach freedom, and a Maryland preacher named Charles Torrey helped some 400 slaves escape.

 Reading Passages

Passengers on the Underground Railroad

Henry "Box" Brown

Henry Brown was a Virginia slave who became famous because of the method he used to escape. He convinced a carpenter friend to build him a box just large enough for him to sit in. He stowed away inside the box with water, a few biscuits, and a tool he used for drilling air holes. The box was nailed shut, and he was shipped by train to Philadelphia, often riding upside-down during the 26-hour journey. When the box was delivered to the Anti-Slavery Society of Philadelphia, they opened it, and Brown emerged—a free man.

Brown often spoke at antislavery meetings, helped others escape along the Underground Railroad, and was even the subject of a song celebrating his escape.

Eliza Harris

Eliza Harris had lost two young children to starvation and mistreatment. When she learned that she and her two-year-old daughter were to be sold to different owners, Harris ran away. Carrying her daughter in her arms, she walked several miles through the bitter cold on a winter night to the Ohio River.

With slave catchers in close pursuit, she leaped onto a piece of ice floating down the river. She jumped to another when that piece started to break apart and sink. Holding her child in her arms, Harris crossed the broad Ohio River by jumping barefoot across broken ice pieces.

A stranger who watched her cross secretly guided Harris to the home of Rev. John Rankin, a prominent member of the Underground Railroad in the mainly antislavery town of Ripley, Ohio. From there she was led to the home of Levi Coffin in Indiana, who moved her along the Underground Railroad to freedom. Author Harriet Beecher Stowe used her story and name in the powerful antislavery novel, *Uncle Tom's Cabin*. Later, Eliza returned to Kentucky to help other members of her family escape.

Anthony Burns

Anthony Burns was a slave hired out to work near the Richmond docks. He convinced a sailor friend to let him stow away on a ship bound for Boston, Massachusetts. He hid in a dark, damp hole in the ship for the three-week voyage. Suffering terribly from cold and hunger, he gritted it out and made it safely to Boston. Burns' owner discovered his whereabouts and arranged for his capture. Despite a public trial which angered many Boston citizens, Burns was forcibly returned to his owner where he was enslaved again until his freedom was purchased by Boston abolitionists.

 Reading Passages

Passengers on the Underground Railroad *(cont.)*

Lear Green

An 18-year-old house slave in Baltimore, Maryland, Lear Green fell in love with a free black man named William Adams. She refused to marry him because she did not want her children to be born as anyone's property.

William arranged with his mother, a free woman, to come to Baltimore from New York. They purchased an old, beaten-up sailor's chest, and Green crawled into it with a pillow, a quilt, some water, and a little food. The chest was loaded onto the deck of a steamer bound for Philadelphia. Because William's mother was not allowed to have a cabin, she got to spend all night next to the chest where she kept an eye on it and talked once or twice to Green.

The chest was delivered to the house of the famous Underground Railroad stationmaster William Still, who was just as astonished to see Green climb out of the chest as he had been when Henry Brown climbed out of his box. Still helped send Green along the network to northern New York, where she joined William's mother and later married William. She only lived two or three more years, but she lived them as a free woman.

Tice Davids

One day in 1831, Tice Davids decided he could no longer live as a slave. He ran away from his owner and headed north to the Ohio River. He hoped to find a small boat he might use to row across the wide

Ohio River, but nothing was there. With his owner in hot pursuit, Tice decided to swim.

Fatigued beyond words, he managed to swim across the fast-flowing and dangerous river while his owner and the slave catchers found a boat and rowed closer and closer. Tice swam to the Ohio shore with the slave catchers right behind him.

His pursuers saw him on shore, but he abruptly vanished, helped by friendly antislavery people. Tice was sent to the small town of Ripley, Ohio, and then moved along the route to freedom in Canada.

Tice's owner tried to find him but said he must have vanished along an "underground railroad" because there was no sign of him. This casual remark by a frustrated slave owner gave rise to the term *Underground Railroad*.

Reading Passages

Passengers on the Underground Railroad *(cont.)*

William and Ellen Craft

William and Ellen Craft attempted one of the longest escapes in the history of slavery. They traveled from Macon, Georgia, in the deep South to Philadelphia, Pennsylvania, on their own.

William and Ellen had been slaves all of their lives. Ellen was a very light-skinned black, the daughter of her owner by one of his slaves. She was hated by her owner's wife, who gave her as a wedding gift to the owner's white daughter.

Ellen met William Craft in Macon but would not marry him at first because neither of them wanted their children to be born as slaves. They decided to escape even though they knew that fugitives in the deep South were usually caught and whipped and often tortured to death. William and Ellen had saved some money from tips and small gifts they received as servants.

Ellen was a very capable seamstress, and William an excellent carpenter whose owner sometimes allowed him to keep a few dollars from the money he earned for his master.

For their escape, Ellen disguised herself as a white man, cut her hair into a masculine style, and covered her face with a bandage to hide her features and indicate a toothache. She wore a wealthy gentleman's suit and hat. Ellen wrapped a sling over her right arm so that she couldn't be forced to write her name because as a slave she was not allowed to learn to read or write.

Ellen could speak with a white accent, and they traveled as William Johnson and slave. Both William and Ellen had obtained passes from their owners to visit relatives for a week at Christmas. By the time they were missed, they hoped to be safe in the North.

They started off by train and were nearly caught immediately by William's master who had become suspicious. Then, Ellen rode in the railroad car right next to a white man she had known for years, who tried to carry on a conversation.

Later on a steamboat to Charlestown, South Carolina, Ellen was berated by a white army officer for spoiling her slave because she let him eat scraps off her plate. He fed her because her arm was supposed to be badly injured. (William had been required to sleep on the deck without food or water as there was no other place for slaves.)

In Charleston, Ellen was challenged by a tough port official who disliked the idea of letting slaves travel North. Unable to even sign her false name on the manifest, they were almost prevented from boarding the steamboat, but the official eventually relented when Ellen got angry with him.

 Reading Passages

Passengers on the Underground Railroad *(cont.)*

William and Ellen Craft *(cont.)*

They traveled by steamboat to Wilmington, North Carolina, and then by train to Richmond, Virginia, where they changed to another train.

At Fredericksburg, Virginia, they boarded a steamboat to Washington, D.C. (still a slave district). Next they took a train to Baltimore, Maryland, where they changed trains again.

Here the journey almost ended because an official said it was illegal to take a slave to Philadelphia (a free state) from Maryland (a slave state). Ellen acted like an arrogant rich man and demanded that they be permitted to proceed because she needed her slave's help. As a result, she got away with it.

Eventually William and Ellen arrived in Philadelphia where they contacted William Still, a famous stationmaster of the Underground Railroad. He hid them for a time and then sent them on to Boston, where they described their adventures and spoke to abolitionist groups.

When their former owners heard about the Crafts' daring escape, they were furious and sent agents to locate them and have them arrested under the terms of the new Fugitive Slave Law, which had just been signed. Believers in the antislavery cause hid the Crafts from federal and state officials, bounty hunters, and slave catchers for a long time.

Finally, the couple boarded a ship for England. Ellen almost died from pneumonia, which she caught while in hiding, and barely survived the trip. They arrived in England on Christmas in 1850, two years after beginning their escape.

The Crafts stayed in England until the Civil War in the United States ended slavery. William and Ellen eventually returned to Georgia, where they opened a school for freed blacks and were widely admired for their generosity.

Reading Passages

The End of the Line

The Campaign Against Slavery

The Underground Railroad was really just one part of the movement to end slavery in the United States. In the early 1800s, the abolitionists who sought to end slavery were few in number, but their persistent and vocal opposition raised Northerners' awareness of the evils of slavery.

Stories detailing the savagery of slave life, told in published slave chronicles and at meetings sponsored by abolitionist leaders, increased Northern opposition to slavery. The stubborn and brutal efforts of the slave owners to defend their "peculiar institution" (slavery) angered leaders in the North and increased public opposition to it.

Warriors for Freedom

The antislavery forces had several well-educated, dynamic, and powerful voices calling for an end to slavery. William Lloyd Garrison was a leading abolitionist who started publishing a newspaper in 1831 named *The Liberator*, which called for an immediate end to slavery. Ralph Waldo Emerson, Wendell Phillips, Louisa May Alcott, and many other New England writers and religious leaders supported the abolitionist cause. James G. Birney was a Southern slaveholder who freed his slaves, became a dedicated abolitionist, and ran for president in 1840 as the Liberty Party candidate.

Frederick Douglass, an escaped slave who later bought his own freedom, became a powerful voice calling for an end to slavery. Sojourner Truth, a former slave, gave speeches opposing slavery throughout the North and West. Wealthy merchants like Lewis and Arthur Tappan provided money and leadership to the cause.

Many abolitionist newspaper publishers were attacked by mobs. Birney had his office destroyed several times and his press hurled into the Ohio River by supporters of slavery. Abolitionist publisher Elijah Lovejoy was killed defending his newspaper.

John Brown Lights a Powder Keg

John Brown was an abolitionist who devoted much of his adult life to the antislavery cause. Brown considered himself an instrument of God, chosen to lead slaves in a revolt against slavery. In October of 1859 he and 21 followers attacked a government armory at Harpers Ferry and called on slaves to revolt against their masters. The uprising never happened, and most of his men were killed. Brown was captured, convicted, and hanged for treason. His actions and statements, however, helped convince many Northerners that slavery had to end. Southerners, on the other hand, realized that compromise was not going to work.

 Reading Passages

The End of the Line *(cont.)*

The Coming of War

With the coming of the Civil War in the United States, the Underground Railroad gradually ceased to operate. Dedicated antislavery advocates kept helping slaves escape during the turbulent years leading up to secession and war. As the conflict turned into war though, more slaves found opportunities to escape. Some Northern generals, however, returned escaping slaves to their owners in keeping with President Abraham Lincoln's efforts to hold the country together and prevent all-out war.

Contraband

Once war began, more and more officers regarded slaves as *contraband*, meaning that slave labor was part of the Confederacy's strength. Helping slaves escape and preventing their return to their owners was a way of reducing the resources of the Confederacy. Union officers decided not to return escaped slaves to their secessionist owners. These actions encouraged more slaves to escape, especially those who lived near Northern states and those who were near Union army camps. The escaped slaves were housed in tents and shacks in makeshift camps and put to work digging trenches, building bridges, and spying for the Northern troops. When the North took possession of the Sea Islands off the coast of South Carolina in November 1861, a huge black population came under the control of the Northern army. Volunteers went South to teach these former slaves and provide them with food, shelter, and the basic necessities of life.

Emancipation Proclamation

In April of 1862, a year after the Civil War began, Congress outlawed slavery in Washington, DC, the nation's capital. In July of that year, Congress authorized the enlistment of black soldiers and volunteers into the military and soon organized many regiments of black troops. By late 1862, President Lincoln had become convinced that the freedom of all slaves was essential. On January 1, 1863, he issued the Emancipation Proclamation which ordered the *emancipation*, or freeing, of all slaves in the seceded states. It did not free the slaves of those loyal to the United States, but it was the beginning of the end of slavery in the U.S.

The Emancipation Proclamation reflected the overwhelming feeling that people in the North had about slavery. Under the terms of the proclamation, about three million slaves were freed. The eventual Union victory in 1865 was followed by the 13th Amendment to the Constitution, which banned the existence of slavery everywhere in the United States. The Underground Railroad had finally reached its ultimate destination—liberty for all slaves.

Beginning of the Underground Railroad Quiz

Directions: Read pages 7–9 about the beginning of the Underground Railroad. Answer each question below by circling the correct answer.

1. When was the term *Underground Railroad* first used?
   a. 1861
   b. 1830
   c. 1820
   d. 1860

2. Who were the abolitionists?
   a. slave owners
   b. slave catchers
   c. opponents of slavery
   d. Canadians

3. How many slaves lived in the South when the Civil War began?
   a. 4 million
   b. 50,000
   c. 5 million
   d. 40,000

4. Under the Fugitive Slave Law of 1850, what was the punishment for those who aided escaping slaves?
   a. $1,000 fine
   b. 6 months in jail
   c. 2 years in jail
   d. both a and b

5. Which state did slaves from Virginia and Maryland often escape to on their way to freedom?
   a. Massachusetts
   b. Vermont
   c. Pennsylvania
   d. Delaware

6. Which of these groups helped *fugitive* slaves?
   a. Quakers
   b. freed blacks
   c. slave catchers
   d. Both a and b

7. What does the word *fugitive* mean?
   a. slave owner
   b. a person fleeing the law
   c. a law officer
   d. a slave

8. Who created a series of hiding places and escape routes for slaves in 1819?
   a. plantation owners
   b. Vestal Coffin
   c. slaves
   d. Congress

9. What guide did fugitive slaves use to travel North?
   a. the North Star
   b. the sun
   c. the moon
   d. Venus

10. Who helped more than 2,500 fugitive slaves escape along the Underground Railroad?
    a. Abraham Lincoln
    b. slave owners
    c. Jefferson Davis
    d. Levi Coffin

Underground Railroad Terms Quiz

Directions: Read page 10, and then complete the crossword puzzle below using the terms in the Word List.

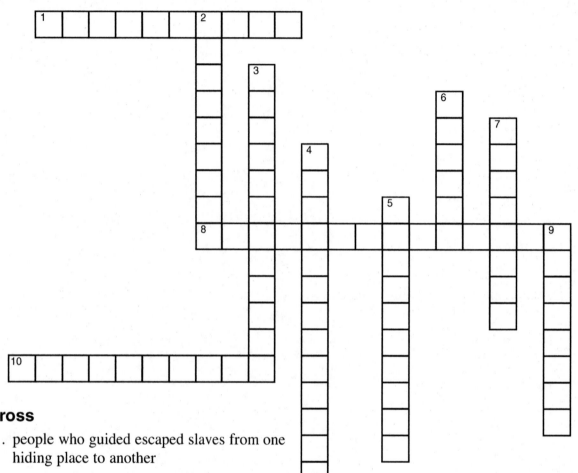

Across

1. people who guided escaped slaves from one hiding place to another
8. those who hid slaves in their homes or farms
10. runaway slaves

Down

2. the end of the line, usually Canada
3. people who opposed slavery and talked slaves into escaping
4. recaptured fugitive slaves
5. a successful escape
6. people who encouraged slaves in the South to escape
7. guides for fugitive slaves in free states
9. hiding places along the route

Word List

brakemen
conductors
passengers
pilots
smooth trip
stationmasters
stations
terminals
ticket agents
train ran off the track

Leaders of the Underground Railroad Quiz

Directions: Read pages 11–14 about the leaders of the Underground Railroad. Answer each question below by circling the correct answer.

1. Which conductor of the Underground Railroad later served with the Union army as spy, scout, and nurse?
   a. William Wells Brown
   b. Harriet Tubman
   c. Levi Coffin
   d. Josiah Henson

2. Who walked more than 400 miles back to Kentucky to rescue the family of his friend, James Lightfoot?
   a. Richard Daly
   b. John Rankin
   c. Levi Coffin
   d. Josiah Henson

3. Who rescued most of her family and over 300 other slaves on 20 trips into the South?
   a. Charity Still
   b. Eliza Harris
   c. Harriet Tubman
   d. John Fairfield

4. Which state offered a $10,000 reward for the capture of Thomas Garret?
   a. Virginia
   b. Delaware
   c. Kentucky
   d. Maryland

5. Which Michigan doctor helped more than 1,500 fugitive slaves?
   a. Charles Torrey
   b. Nathan Thomas
   c. Jonathan Walker
   d. Richard Daly

6. Which Philadelphia leader discovered that one of his "passengers" was his own long-lost brother, Peter?
   a. William Still
   b. Jonathan Parker
   c. Richard Daly
   d. John Fairfield

7. Who hid Eliza Harris in his home, helped her escape, and then helped her return to Kentucky to find her other children?
   a. Levi Coffin
   b. Harriet Tubman
   c. John Rankin
   d. Jonathan Walker

8. Who helped disguise slaves when they stopped at her home?
   a. Catherine Coffin
   b. Harriet Tubman
   c. Eliza Harris
   d. John Parker

9. Who rowed many fugitive slaves across the Ohio River?
   a. John Rankin
   b. John Parker
   c. William Still
   d. Thomas Garrett

10. Which Delaware Quaker lost all of his possessions to pay fines for helping fugitive slaves escape?
    a. Thomas Garrett
    b. Levi Coffin
    c. John Rankin
    d. John Fairfield

Passengers on the Underground Railroad Quiz

Directions: Read pages 15–18 about the passengers of the Underground Railroad. Answer each question below by circling the correct answer.

1. Which fugitive slave was a stowaway on a ship to Boston and later recaptured and returned to slavery?
   a. Anthony Burns
   b. Lear Green
   c. Tice Davids
   d. William Craft

2. Which woman traveled North disguised as a white man?
   a. Eliza Harris
   b. Ellen Craft
   c. Harriet Tubman
   d. Lear Green

3. Which slave's successful escape gave rise to the term *Underground Railroad*?
   a. Anthony Burns
   b. Tice Davids
   c. Henry Brown
   d. William Craft

4. Who used the story of Eliza Harris's escape in her novel?
   a. Harriet Tubman
   b. Ellen Craft
   c. Lear Green
   d. Harriet Beecher Stowe

5. Who wrapped her arm in a sling to hide her ability to write?
   a. Ellen Craft
   b. Lear Green
   c. Eliza Harris
   d. Harriet Tubman

6. Who shipped himself to freedom in a box?
   a. Anthony Burns
   b. William Craft
   c. Henry Brown
   d. Tice Davids

7. Who was shipped to a free state in a sailor's chest?
   a. Henry Brown
   b. Eliza Harris
   c. Lear Green
   d. Margaret Garner

8. Who escaped from Georgia to Philadelphia to Boston to England?
   a. William Craft
   b. Eliza Harris
   c. Ellen Craft
   d. both a and c

9. Who jumped barefoot across broken patches of river ice with her child in her arms?
   a. Eliza Harris
   b. Ellen Craft
   c. Margaret Garner
   d. Lear Green

10. Who helped William and Ellen Craft hide and then get from Philadelphia to Boston?
    a. Levi Coffin
    b. William Still
    c. Anthony Burns
    d. John Rankin

The End of the Line Quiz

Directions: Read pages 19 and 20 about the end of the Underground Railroad. Answer each question below by circling the correct answer.

1. Who escaped from slavery and later bought his freedom?
   a. Sojourner Truth
   b. Frederick Douglass
   c. John Brown
   d. James Birney

2. Which group of people sought to end slavery by speaking and writing against its evils?
   a. Southerners
   b. Congress
   c. slave owners
   d. abolitionists

3. What does the word *emancipate* mean?
   a. to enslave
   b. to protest
   c. to free
   d. to enlist in the army

4. What word was used by Union officers to indicate slaves?
   a. emancipation
   b. contraband
   c. abolitionist
   d. treason

5. Which of these people was killed defending his abolitionist newspaper?
   a. Elijah Lovejoy
   b. Sojourner Truth
   c. William Lloyd Garrison
   d. John Brown

6. Which Southern slaveholder freed his slaves, became an abolitionist, and ran for president in 1840?
   a. Abraham Lincoln
   b. James Birney
   c. John Brown
   d. Elijah Lovejoy

7. When was slavery outlawed in Washington, DC?
   a. 1840
   b. 1800
   c. 1862
   d. 1865

8. Who attacked Harpers Ferry and called for a slave revolt?
   a. Frederick Douglass
   b. James Birney
   c. John Brown
   d. Abraham Lincoln

9. Which of these people was **not** an abolitionist?
   a. Abraham Lincoln
   b. James Birney
   c. Louisa May Alcott
   d. Elijah Lovejoy

10. Union officers did not want to return slaves to their owners because slaves
   a. were opposed to slavery.
   b. would reveal army secrets.
   c. fought well.
   d. were part of the South's power.

1650   1700   1750   1800   1850   1900

Teacher Lesson Plans for Language Arts

Novels and Biographies

Objectives: Students will read from and respond to novels and biographies based on the experiences of people involved in the abolition of slavery and/or the Underground Railroad.

Materials: copies of Elements of a Novel (pages 27 and 28); copies of Biographies (pages 29 and 30); copies of Harriet Tubman (page 31); copies of novels based on the Underground Railroad (see pages 28 and 46); copies of biographies about slaves and abolitionists (see pages 30 and 46); biographies on Harriet Tubman (page 31)

Procedure

1. Reproduce and distribute Elements of a Novel. Help students choose appropriate novels. Have students complete Assignment 1 and/or Assignment 2.

2. Reproduce and distribute the Biographies pages. Help students choose appropriate biographies. After they have read the books, instruct them to complete the Biographical Outline on page 29. In small groups or as a class, discuss the people that students read about using the questions at the bottom of page 30.

3. Reproduce and distribute the Harriet Tubman activity page. Help students choose appropriate biographies about her. Have them write about Harriet's life using the biographical outline on page 29 as a guide. Discuss the questions on page 31 together.

Assessment: Use student outlines, class discussions, and writing assignments to assess students' performance on the literature selections.

Readers' Theater

Objective: Students will learn to use their voices effectively in dramatic reading.

Materials: copies of Readers' Theater Notes (page 32); copies of Moses Leads Her People to Freedom (pages 33 and 34); copies of Stealing Freedom (pages 35–38)

Procedure

1. Review the basic concept of readers' theater with the class, using the Readers' Theater Notes to emphasize important skills.

2. Have students read Moses Leads Her People to Freedom and Stealing Freedom. Place students in small groups, assign them one of the scripts, and allow time for them to practice reading it over several days.

3. Schedule class performances, and have students share these prepared scripts.

4. As an extension, students can write and perform their own scripts about the Underground Railroad.

Assessment: Base performance assessments on participants' pacing, volume, expression, and focus. Student-created scripts should demonstrate general writing skills, dramatic tension, and a good plot.

1650   1700   1750   1800   1850   1900

Elements of a Novel

Assignment 1

Read a novel about the Underground Railroad. Several are listed on page 28. Complete the outline below. Then share the information with a small group or the entire class.

Story Outline

Book Title: _____

Genre (historical fiction, fantasy, contemporary realism): _____

Setting of the story (where and when): _____

Protagonist (one or two facts about the central character): _____

Major characters (include one or two descriptive facts about each): _____

_____

Lesser characters (include one or two descriptive facts about each): _____

_____

Point of view (Is the story told in first person or third person?): _____

Plot (3–6 sentences about the story line): _____

_____

_____

_____

_____

Problem/Conflict (basic problem in one sentence): _____

_____

Climax (story's turning point): _____

_____

Resolution (how the story ends): _____

_____

Feeling/Tone (book's general tone—depressing, uplifting, sad, funny, etc.): _____

Theme (ideas the story addresses, such as good versus evil): _____

_____

Personal evaluation (your response to the characters and story): _____

_____

_____

©Teacher Created Resources, Inc.   27   #3215 Underground Railroad

Elements of a Novel *(cont.)*

Assignment 2

Read one of the novels about the Underground Railroad that is listed at the bottom of the page. When finished, complete one of the following writing assignments.

- **Character Sketch**

  Write a character sketch describing a major character in the book. Emphasize the character's traits, personality, and any significant events that changed his or her life.

- **Library Brochure**

  Write a brochure telling about a novel you read and why you recommend it. Illustrate it and then give a copy to the school or public library.

- **Personal Response to Literature**

  Write a personal evaluation of the novel giving your response to one character and what happened to that person. Include your personal feelings as you read the book as well as any lessons you learned from the person.

- **Summary**

  Write a summary of a novel, describing the main events that occurred.

- **Villain**

  Choose a character in the novel who is a villain or a disagreeable person. Describe the behavior and personality traits of this individual, giving specific examples of what he or she said or did.

Novels About the Underground Railroad

Greenwood, Barbara. *The Last Safe House: A Story of the Underground Railroad*. Kids Can Press, 1998. (An easy-to-read story of an escaped slave child and the family who protect her from slave catchers)

Houston, Gloria. *Bright Freedom's Song*. Harcourt Brace, 1998. (A fast-paced novel of a teenage girl's commitment to runaway slaves at her family's station on the Underground Railroad)

Lyons, Mary E. *Letters From a Slave Girl: The Story of Harriet Jacobs*. Scribners, 1992. (A novelized account of a fugitive slave who wrote her own memoirs of her life as a slave)

Pearsall, Shelley. *Trouble Don't Last*. Dell, 2002. (An exciting, award-winning novel depicting the run to freedom of an old slave and a young boy)

Rinaldi, Ann. *Numbering All the Bones*. Scholastic, 2002. (A powerful story of a slave girl torn between loyalty to her slave family and her desire for freedom)

Rinaldi, Ann. *Taking Liberty: The Story of Oney Judge, George Washington's Runaway Slave*. Simon & Schuster, 2002. (The life of a girl who chose freedom despite many hardships and personal conflicts)

1650   1700   1750   1800   1850   1900

Biographies

A *biography* tells the true life story of a person. There are many biographies written about fugitive slaves, leaders of the Underground Railroad, and abolitionists who opposed slavery. Frederick Douglass wrote a famous *autobiography* (the story of his own life), which convinced many readers that slavery was evil. Some escaped slaves wrote or dictated slave chronicles that described their lives of suffering and oppression. (See page 46.)

Assignment

Choose a person you admire from the list on page 30. Read a biography about that person or a book about the lives of several people (listed on the next page or in the school or public library). Use the outline below to help you research important information about the person, and take notes on index cards. Then write a biographical essay about the person.

Biographical Outline

I. Youth

   A. Birth place and date (if known)

   B. Home life and family life

      1. Parents

      2. Brothers and sisters

      3. Place lived (significant events)

      4. Spouse and children

   C. Schooling (if any)

   D. Interesting facts and stories

II. Adult life

   A. Experiences with slavery

   B. Opposition to slavery

      1. Influential people in his/her life

      2. Significant events

      3. Involvement in the Underground Railroad

      4. Dangers faced

III. Death

   A. Date and place

   B. Age

   C. Cause

©*Teacher Created Resources, Inc.*   29   *#3215 Underground Railroad*

Biographies *(cont.)*

Slaves and Abolitionists

Alexander Ross—He went South from Canada to find passengers.

Anthony Burns—He was called the "Boston Lion."

Dred Scott—He sued for freedom but lost.

Elijah Lovejoy—His press could be stopped but not silenced.

Eliza Harris—Her escape inspired Harriet Beecher Stowe.

Frederick Douglass—He "stole himself."

Harriet Beecher Stowe—She wrote *Uncle Tom's Cabin*.

Henry Brown—He escaped in a box.

James Birney—He rejected slavery.

John Parker—He guided slaves across the Ohio River.

John Rankin—He was a true believer in God and freedom.

Levi Coffin—He was the "Grand Central Stationmaster."

Sojourner Truth—She went from being a slave to helping slaves to freedom.

Thomas Garrett—He was "chief operator of the Eastern line."

Tice Davids—His escape created the term *Underground Railroad*.

William Still—He was the Philadelphia connection.

Biographies About Slaves

Cooper, Michael L. *From Slave to Civil War Hero: The Life and Times of Robert Smalls.* (The exciting story of a fugitive slave who stole a Confederate ship and sailed it to freedom along with a slave crew and their families)

Fradin, Dennis Brindell. *Bound for the North Star: True Stories of the Fugitive Slaves.* Clarion, 2000. (Vivid, well-written accounts of escape attempts by fugitive slaves)

Hamilton, Virginia. *Many Thousand Gone: African Americans from Slavery to Freedom.* Knopf, 1993. (Excellent overview of the resistance to slavery)

McPherson, Stephanie S. *Sisters Against Slavery: A Story about Sarah and Angelina Grimke.* Carolrhoda, 1999. (An easy biography detailing the story of two Southern-born sisters who grew up to hate and oppose the evils of slavery)

Discussion Questions

Discuss the following questions in small groups or with the entire class.

1. How and why was the person you read about important?
2. How did the experiences in this person's youth affect his or her adult life?
3. What experiences, events, people, or ideas caused this person to oppose slavery?
4. What leadership qualities did this person demonstrate?
5. Would you have liked to have known this person? Why?
6. How did this person display courage, loyalty, and honor?
7. What did this person accomplish in his or her life?
8. What was the greatest challenge this person faced?

Harriet Tubman

The person most closely associated with the Underground Railroad is Harriet Tubman. Harriet's determination to rescue her family and other slaves, her gritty courage, and her unwavering belief that all slaves should be free made her a symbol of liberty to the repressed slaves and to all people opposed to slavery. To Southern slave owners, Harriet was a symbol of danger, threatening their control of the slaves which they viewed as valuable "property."

Assignment

Read a biography about Harriet Tubman. Choose from the list at the bottom of this page or another one that is available. Use the biographical outline on page 29 to write a biographical sketch of her life. Discuss the following questions in small groups or with the entire class.

Discussion Questions

1. Describe Harriet's childhood. Were there any happy moments in her life?

2. What was Harriet's attitude toward being a slave? Was she angry, obedient, quiet, happy, etc.?

3. How did Harriet's family encourage her desire for freedom?

4. How did the violent act of the overseer affect Harriet's entire life?

5. What things did Harriet learn as a child that helped her escape? What things did Harriet not know that made escape more difficult?

6. What help did Harriet receive when she escaped from slavery?

7. Why did Harriet's husband refuse to leave with her?

8. Why was William Still opposed at first to Harriet's desire to go back and rescue her family in the South?

9. Describe some of the adventures Harriet had on her journeys into slave states.

10. What services did Harriet provide during the Civil War to help end slavery?

11. How would you describe the character of Harriet Tubman?

Biographies About Harriet Tubman

Carlson, Judy. *Harriet Tubman: Call to Freedom.* Fawcett, 1989. (An excellent account of Harriet's life and work for middle-graders)

Sterling, Dorothy. *The Story of Harriet Tubman: Freedom Train.* Scholastic, 1954. (A complete, easy-to-read biography of this great conductor)

Readers' Theater Notes

Readers' Theater is drama without costumes, props, stage, or memorization. It can be done in the classroom by groups of students, who become the cast of the dramatic reading.

Staging

Place chairs, desks, or stools in a semicircle at the front of the class or in a separate staging area. Generally no costumes are used in this type of dramatization, but students dressed in similar clothing or colors add a nice effect. Simple props can be used but are not required.

Scripting

Each member of the group should have a clearly marked script. Performers should practice several times before presenting the play to the class.

Performing

Performers should enter the classroom quietly and seriously. They should sit silently without moving and wait with their heads lowered. The first reader should begin, and the other readers should focus on whoever is reading, except when they are performing. If desired, actors can use accents, mime, or movement to add a more dramatic effect.

Assignment

Read one of the readers' theater scripts in this book: Moses Leads Her People to Freedom (pages 33 and 34) about Harriet Tubman or Stealing Freedom (pages 35–38) about the dramatic escape of William and Mary Craft. Working with a small group, practice the script. Then perform the play for the rest of the class.

Extension

Write your own Readers' Theater script based on one of the events listed below or another topic related to the Underground Railroad. Practice your script with classmates, and then perform it for the class.

- Henry "Box" Brown ships himself to freedom.

- Thomas Garrett loses everything he owns helping runaway slaves.

- Harriet Tubman makes one of her 19 trips into slave territory to rescue fugitive slaves.

- Anthony Burns is recaptured and returned to slavery.

- Eliza Harris crosses the Ohio River with her child in her arms.

- Levi Coffin welcomes a fugitive slave family.

- Lear Green hides in a trunk and is shipped to freedom.

Readers' Theater: Moses Leads Her People to Freedom

This script is an account of one of Harriet Tubman's trips to the South to free other slaves. There are six speaking parts.

Narrator: In 1849 Harriet Tubman learned that she was about to be sold so she decided to escape while she was still in Maryland, next to the free state of Pennsylvania. She left her husband, who was unwilling to go with her, and traveled by foot mostly at night. She made contact with stationmasters of the Underground Railroad who guided her to Philadelphia. There she met William Still, a leading member of the antislavery society, who helped her get settled.

Harriet: I have a job and my freedom, Mr. Still, but it isn't enough. My brothers and sister, parents, and friends are still human property. There are more than three million of my people in slavery. I must go down South, like Moses, to bring my people to freedom.

William Still: I understand your dedication, Harriet, but all of our conductors are men. Going South is terribly dangerous. You are a fugitive. Once you cross the line, you are a slave again. The slave catchers and patrollers are brutal men. They get paid for you whether you are dead or alive.

Harriet: Nobody cared I wasn't a man when they tied me to a mule to plow the fields or put an ax in my hands. I have a pistol. I don't intend to get caught, and I won't be taken alive. I have saved a few dollars, and as soon as I have enough, I plan to go back for my family. Can you find out anything about them through your contacts in Maryland?

Narrator: William Still discovered that Harriet's sister, Mary Ann, was to be sold at an auction. Harriet traveled back to Maryland, going from one Underground Railroad station to another. She arrived in Cambridge, Maryland, armed with her pistol and a great deal of courage. She met Mary Ann's husband, John Bowley, a free black, in a barn.

John Bowley: Harriet, I'm so happy to see you, but they already have Mary and our three children in the slave pens. The auctioneer is going to sell them this afternoon.

Harriet: Wait until the auctioneer goes to lunch. Write a note saying that these four slaves were bought by a wealthy planter and that you are to take them to him. The guards will not expect a forgery. Slaves aren't supposed to read or write. Bring them to the old farm house at the edge of town. They're friends. Hide there until night.

Readers' Theater: Moses Leads Her People to Freedom *(cont.)*

Mary Ann: The sky's overcast. How are we going to find the Drinking Gourd to point us North? We could get lost.

Harriet: No, our father taught us that the moss grows on the north side of the tree. We can feel the trees.

Narrator: By the time they had traveled a few miles on foot, Mary Ann's youngest child was fussy, and one of the fugitive slaves with them was beginning to complain.

Harriet: Mary Ann, give this medicine to Annie. We can't afford to have her crying. Sound carries a long way in the woods.

Mary Ann: Do we have to? Will it hurt her?

Harriet: It's a sleeping potion. She'll be fine. We can't take chances.

Slave: Are you sure you know where we're going? If we go back now, they may never know we left. I don't want to get caught. I'm heading back.

Narrator: Harriet draws her pistol from her bag and points it at the men.

Harriet: Nobody leaves. Nobody quits. You endanger us all if you do. Believe me, I'll shoot anyone who runs. We're bound for freedom, and there's no turning back.

Narrator: They arrived at a dirt cellar near the edge of a field of potatoes.

Harriet: We stay in this potato cellar tonight. No talking. It's going to be very crowded. There's barely room for us to fit, but it won't be the worst. Tomorrow we travel in a wagon under a load of hay. We will be hiding in attics and barns and in a tunnel near a ditch. It's a long way, but we will make it.

Narrator: They traveled for a week from one station to another along a network of farms, Quaker meeting houses, and abandoned sheds until they reached the safety of Philadelphia and William Still's home. Mary Ann and her family were sent north to Canada, and Harriet headed back South after a few months to rescue more of her family. Harriet Tubman made 20 trips into slave states to bring her family, friends, and other slaves to freedom. She became known as "Moses" to the people she helped. She was so feared by slave owners that they offered a $40,000 bounty for her—dead or alive.

Readers' Theater: Stealing Freedom

This script tells of the escape of William and Ellen Craft from Macon, Georgia, to Philadelphia, Pennsylvania. There are seven speaking parts. Some speakers can perform two roles.

Narrator: William and Ellen Craft lived in Macon, Georgia, in the deep South. They had been slaves all of their lives. Ellen was a very light-skinned black slave. She was the daughter of her owner and one of his slaves. She was given as a wedding gift to the owner's white daughter who lived in Macon, Georgia. Ellen grew up as a household servant and became a skilled seamstress. Sometimes she earned small tips for her work. When Ellen was 18, she met William, a talented carpenter who worked in a cabinet shop. Although he was a slave, William's owner allowed him to keep a little of his pay. He also earned small tips in other odd jobs. William and Ellen decided to marry.

Ellen: William, I love you deeply, but we must get out of this place before we have children. I don't want my children born as slaves and owned by my master. I won't have it.

William: My first owner sold my parents to different planters. I never saw them again nor did they see each other ever again. My brothers and sisters were each sold to different slave buyers as I was growing up. Right now I have a better owner than most slaves do, but he could sell me tomorrow. I could be led away in chains to work hundreds of miles away, and I'd be forever separated from you. Our only hope is freedom, and I think I have a plan that will work.

Ellen: We have to escape, but Macon, is hundreds of miles from any Northern state. We could be caught by bounty hunters or slave catchers before we reach the Ohio River and the free states north of it. We don't know the way, and we would be alone against the world with no one to help us. We'd never survive alone in the mountains, swamps, or wild regions like some slaves have done.

William: Runaways hardly ever make it from as far South as we live. They are usually caught, whipped, attacked by dogs, branded, sold farther South to cotton farmers, or tortured to death.

Ellen: What is your plan, William?

William: Take me North on the train as your slave.

Ellen: What are you talking about?

William: I've been thinking this out very carefully for some time. I'm dark skinned, and nothing will disguise my looks. But you are light-skinned and could almost pass for being white.

Readers' Theater: Stealing Freedom (cont.)

Ellen: Maybe in the dark, but I'd quickly be discovered. White men would notice the difference. I don't look that much like a white woman, and even a white woman traveling with a slave would have trouble going where she wanted to when we got close to the Northern states.

William: True, but a white man with his slave would hardly be noticed. You would have to cut your beautiful hair into a white man's style and wear some men's clothes. Your face is too soft and womanly so we'd have to hide it somehow.

Ellen: A toothache! Old man Carothers has had a bandage over his face for a month. It would hide most of my face. I can't read or write though, and travelers have to sign their names on ship manifests and other documents. We aren't even allowed to learn how to write our own names, but I can talk like a white. I used to imitate all of the white people when I was growing up.

William: You could have a broken arm or a serious disease and carry your right arm in a sling. Then you couldn't be expected to write. It would also give you an excuse to keep your slave with you.

Ellen: This may work. But when we start, William, I'm not turning back. I'd rather die like a dog than be brought back. We go together—all the way to freedom . . . or death!

William: All the way to freedom or death. We will steal ourselves and our freedom. The best time to leave is at Christmas. White folks are distracted at that time of the year.

Narrator: Ellen made a man's suit, and both slaves got Christmas passes from their owners allowing them to stay with family for a few days. They traveled as William Johnson and his slave. By the time they were missed, they hoped to be safe in the North. They boarded the train just before Christmas and walked into danger almost immediately. As a slave, William had to ride in the baggage car. While sitting in a corner of the car, he saw his master checking every railroad car searching for him. His master had become suspicious and was checking to make sure he hadn't run away on the train. Ellen, in the meantime, had problems of her own. A white man she had known for years sat down next to her in the passenger compartment.

Train Passenger: Where are you traveling, sir, at this time of year? You don't look well.

Readers' Theater: Stealing Freedom *(cont.)*

Ellen: (Her voice is muffled by the bandage.) I'm traveling to Virginia to meet relatives. I've never been there. I have a terrible toothache. I've had it for weeks. I fell and cut my arm and hit my jaw. I haven't felt right since.

Train Passenger: I know a good doctor at our next stop. Perhaps you should stop and see him.

Ellen: I think not. I'll see my family's doctor in Virginia when I get there. I'm going to just rest now.

Train Passenger: Suit yourself.

Narrator: They left the train and boarded a steamboat bound for Charlestown, South Carolina. Ellen let William eat scraps off her plate. He was feeding her because her arm was supposed to be badly injured. William was required to sleep on the deck without food or water as there was no other place for slaves.

Army Officer: You're spoiling that slave, you know. You treat him like a favored child or pet. These blacks need to be kept in their place.

Ellen: I'm not feeling well. My arm is hurt, and he feeds me.

Army Officer: That's all well and good, but you're letting that slave eat the scraps off your own plate. That's disgusting! He'll forget his place. Slaves need to be whipped good and often. I'd be glad to give him a good thrashing right now if you'd like. It would teach him a lesson.

Ellen: I can handle my own business and my own slaves without any interference from you, thank you.

Army Officer: You're making a mistake. Take my word for it. Next thing you know, he'll be running away to the North. Tell you what. I'll give you a $1,000 for that slave right now. I could use one of his size to handle the horses, and you won't have to worry about him escaping. I'll teach him some. . .

Ellen: No, he's been in my family a long time. He's trusted, and I need him.

Army Officer: Pity. You're making a big mistake.

Ellen: I don't think so.

Narrator: In Charleston, Ellen was challenged by a tough port official who disliked the idea of letting slaves travel North. Ellen lets her anger work for her.

Readers' Theater: Stealing Freedom *(cont.)*

Port Official: Sir, you can't take that slave on the steamboat, and you don't want to. You're heading into free states, and that slave is likely to just up and run away.

Ellen: William has been with my family a long time. I need him.

Port Official: I can't let you take him. There are too many runaway slaves in the North, and you haven't signed the manifest.

Ellen: I can't sign. My arm is broken. I paid for our passage, and I'm boarding the ship. I am a Southern gentleman. I have urgent business in Washington, and I will not have my business interfered with. Now get us on that ship!

Port Official: All right, sir. I'll let you board, but mind my words. That slave will be up North and free in a week.

Narrator: William and Ellen sailed by steamboat to Wilmington, North Carolina, and then rode trains to Richmond and Fredericksburg, Virginia. They boarded a steamboat to Washington, DC, and rode a train to Baltimore, Maryland, where they switched trains for the trip to Philadelphia. Here they were stopped by a determined railroad agent.

Railroad Agent: Mister, you can't take that slave with you to Philadelphia. It's a hiding place for fugitive slaves. He'll run away as soon as he sets foot in the city, or some abolitionist will turn his head with radical ideas. He can't go.

Ellen: I am ill, and I need William's help. He has always been very loyal.

Railroad Agent: You can't trust any slave. They'll all run at the first chance. I'll not allow him to travel on the train.

Ellen: I come from one of the best families in Georgia. I paid for my ticket. William will ride in the baggage car as usual. We are going on this train, or I'll contact higher authorities!

Railroad Agent: Okay, but you've been warned. You better keep a chain on that fellow, or he'll be free in no time.

Narrator: She got away with it. William and Ellen arrived in Philadelphia where they contacted William Still, a famous stationmaster of the Underground Railroad. He hid them for a few weeks and then sent them on to Boston, but their masters found out where they were and had them followed. Two years after William and Ellen started their journey, they sailed to England, where they remained until the end of the Civil War.

Teacher Lesson Plans for Social Studies and Science

Using Time Lines

Objectives: Students will derive information from a time line and make visual time lines.

Materials: copies of Time Line of the Underground Railroad (page 40); reference materials including books, encyclopedias, atlases; colored pencils or markers; white rolled paper (shelf paper, fax rolls, etc.)

Procedure

1. Collect reference materials so students have plenty of resources to find information.
2. Review the concept of a time line, using events from the school year as examples.
3. Reproduce and distribute Time Line of the Underground Railroad. Review each event.
4. Instruct students to complete the assignment, adding additional dates to the time line and creating a visual time line as described on the page.

Assessment: Have students share their visual time lines with their additional dates.

Using Maps

Objective: Students will learn to use and derive information from maps.

Materials: copies of Map of Free and Slave States (page 41); copies of Map of Slave Escape Routes (page 42)

Procedure

1. Review the Map of Free and Slave States with students and make sure that students are able to read the map key. Assign the activity on the page.
2. Review the Map of Slave Escape Routes. Have students use the map to complete the activity.

Assessment: Correct the map activities with students. Check for understanding.

Making Science Models

Objectives: Students will learn about the constellations by creating simple models.

Materials: copies of Drinking Gourd (pages 43 and 44); materials listed including a small hammer, small nails, flashlight, markers, tin cans or round salt boxes, wire clothes hangers, small adhesive stars, clear tape, blue stretchable plastic wrap

Procedure

1. Collect the materials listed before starting each project.
2. Reproduce and distribute the Drinking Gourd pages.
3. Distribute the materials for the Miniature Constellation activity. Review the directions to make a tin can constellation. Allow students time to make and then demonstrate their models in a darkened classroom. (**Note:** *Adult supervision is needed for this activity.*)
4. Distribute the materials to make a Constellation Mobile. Review the directions, and have students construct a clothes-hanger constellation. Display these in the classroom if desired.

Assessment: Have students share their models with the class.

Time Line of the Underground Railroad

1793—The first Fugitive Slave Law is passed, making it illegal to help runaway slaves.

1808—Congress forbids black slaves being imported to the U.S.

1819—The probable date for the first Underground Railroad organization, set up by Vestal Coffin.

1820—The Missouri Compromise is passed to maintain a balance between slave and free states.

1826—Levi Coffin sets up an Underground Railroad station in Newport, Indiana.

1831—Tice Davids' escape across the Ohio leads to the term *Underground Railroad*.

1838—Frederick Douglass escapes from slavery.

1839—Levi Coffin sets up another home station in Liberty, Indiana.

1848—Thomas Garrett is convicted and fined for violating the Fugitive Slave Law.

Ellen and William Craft begin their long journey to freedom, disguised as master and slave.

1849—Harriet Tubman escapes from her owner in Maryland.

Henry "Box" Brown ships himself to freedom.

1850—A more repressive Fugitive Slave Law is passed with tough fines and punishments.

Lear Green travels in a sailor's chest to Philadelphia.

1851—Harriet Tubman makes the first of 19 trips into slave states, which will eventually bring more than 300 slaves to freedom.

1852—*Uncle Tom's Cabin* is written by Harriet Beecher Stowe and has a powerful effect on public opposition to slavery in the North.

1859—John Brown and 21 of his followers occupy Harpers Ferry and call for a slave uprising.

1860—Thomas Garrett is killed during a slave uprising.

Abraham Lincoln is elected president of the United States.

1861—Confederate troops fire on Fort Sumter in Charleston, South Carolina, beginning the Civil War.

1862—Slavery is abolished in Washington, DC.

1863—Lincoln issues the Emancipation Proclamation, freeing slaves in rebel states.

1865—The 13th Amendment to the Constitution is passed, abolishing slavery in the U.S.

Assignment

Use books and other reference materials to find at least 10 dates in American history to add to the time line above. These dates can include wars, inventions, presidential elections, disasters, or sporting events. Then create a visual time line writing these facts on a roll of shelf paper, perforated computer paper, fax rolls, or small adding machine rolls. Mark squares or rectangles with a ruler, and write the date and the event at the top of the square. In the lower half of the square, draw a picture to illustrate each event. Use colored pencils or markers to color each illustration.

Map of Free and Slave States

This map of the United States in 1863 shows which states allowed slavery and the states which did not. It also shows eight territories that had not yet become states.

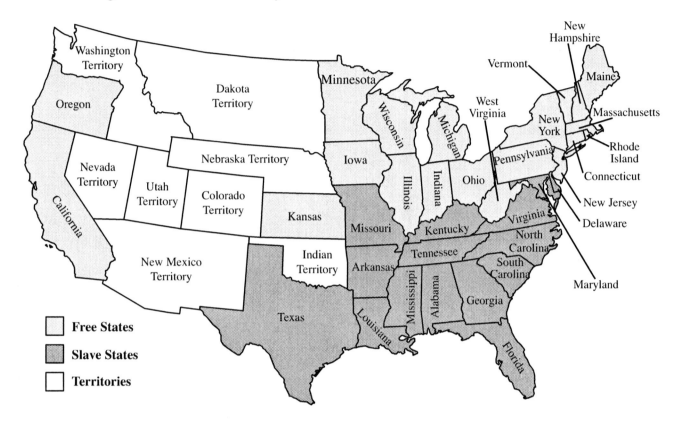

Directions: List the 15 slave states.

1. _____   6. _____   11. _____
2. _____   7. _____   12. _____
3. _____   8. _____   13. _____
4. _____   9. _____   14. _____
5. _____   10. _____   15. _____

Directions: List the 20 free states.

1. _____   8. _____   15. _____
2. _____   9. _____   16. _____
3. _____   10. _____   17. _____
4. _____   11. _____   18. _____
5. _____   12. _____   19. _____
6. _____   13. _____   20. _____
7. _____   14. _____

Map of Slave Escape Routes

Fugitive slaves tried to take the most direct route to freedom. Usually this involved heading North, but some slaves from the deep South tried to reach Mexico, the Bahamas, Cuba, or England. Many tried to stow away on ships headed for free ports. This map shows the routes taken by runaway slaves.

Directions: Use the above map to answer the following questions.

1. Which three states having many Underground Railroad stations did fugitive slaves from Kentucky, Tennessee, and Arkansas try to reach on their journey to freedom?

2. What was the first state that runaways from Virginia tried to reach?

3. Which two states did fugitives from the Carolinas and Georgia try to reach by ship?

4. Which states bordered Canada and were on the route of the Underground Railroad?

5. Which island areas did many fugitive slaves from Florida try to reach?

Drinking Gourd

Runaway slaves knew that the Big Dipper, which they called the "Drinking Gourd," points to the North Star. The Big Dipper is part of a constellation known as Ursa Major. With these reliable stars to guide them, runaway slaves headed North to freedom by following the Drinking Gourd.

Miniature Constellation

Follow the instructions below to make a model of a miniature constellation. (**Note:** *Adult supervision is needed for this activity.*)

Materials

small hammer   marker

small nails   tin can or round, cardboard salt box

flashlight   constellation pictures on page 44

Procedure

1. Use a marker to mark the outline of the stars in one constellation onto the end of a can.

2. Use a hammer and nail to punch a hole in the can at each star marked.

3. Darken the room, and shine a flashlight through the can onto a blank wall. An outline of the constellation will appear. For best results, hold the flashlight at an angle inside the can.

Constellation Mobile

Follow the instructions below to make a mobile of a constellation.

Materials

wire clothes hanger

small, colored adhesive stars

clear cellophane tape

2 feet of blue, stretchable plastic wrap

constellation pictures on page 44

Procedure

1. Bend the wire hanger to form a four-sided figure.

2. Wrap a 2-foot piece of blue plastic wrap around the wire hanger so that the hanger is tightly covered on both sides. Tape the film firmly in place along the bottom of the hanger.

3. Arrange the adhesive stars in the form of a constellation as shown on page 44, and display the mobile.

1650   1700   1750   1800   1850   1900

Drinking Gourd *(cont.)*

Directions: Use these constellation pictures with the activities on page 43.

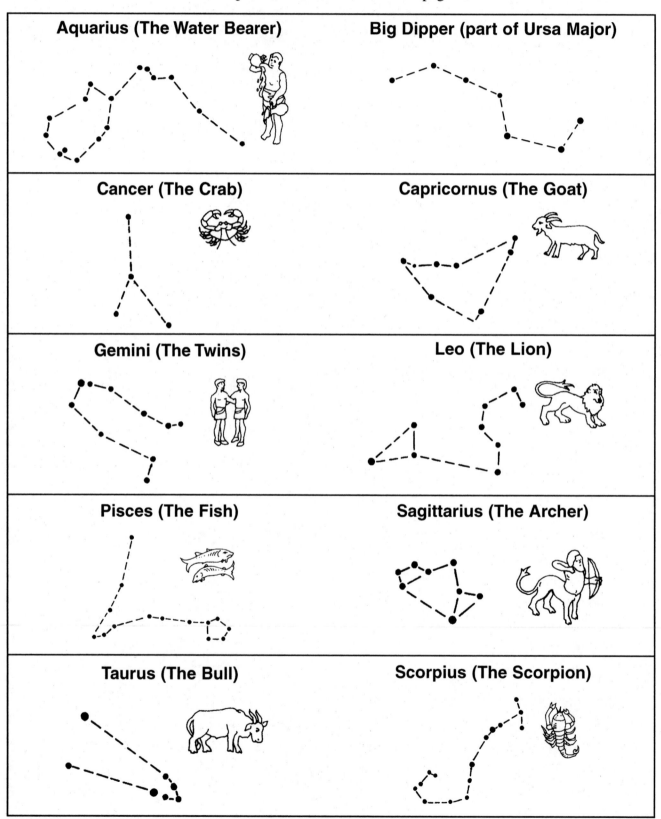

Aquarius (The Water Bearer)

Big Dipper (part of Ursa Major)

Cancer (The Crab)

Capricornus (The Goat)

Gemini (The Twins)

Leo (The Lion)

Pisces (The Fish)

Sagittarius (The Archer)

Taurus (The Bull)

Scorpius (The Scorpion)

Culminating Activities

Set aside one day to be devoted to activities related to your study of the Underground Railroad. If possible, do this with one or two other classes at the same grade level. This allows you to share some of the responsibilities and provides a special experience for students. Encourage parents or family members to come for all or part of the day to enjoy the proceedings and to help set up and monitor the activities. Check with parents to discover any special talents, interests, or hobbies that would be a match for specific centers.

Eat Hearty

If you have parent volunteers, plan a luncheon with a country theme or one that highlights popular foods of the time. Have students make table decorations at one of the centers. Make sure students do not have any food allergies or dietary restrictions.

Centers

The centers you set up should relate in some way to the Civil War, daily life during this time period, or activities from this book. Centers should involve small groups of six or seven students doing an activity and/or making something they can display. Each center should take about 20 minutes after which time students can rotate to the next activity. The following are suggestions for various centers, or you may add others for which you have special expertise.

☐ **Reenact the Escapes**

Have students use the information they have learned from this book to reenact some of the famous escapes they read about. Each group could use the classroom or an outdoor area to reenact the escapes of Harriet Tubman and her many journeys into slave territory, the river crossing of Eliza Harris, the adventures of John Parker, or the escape of Ellen and William Craft among many others. Assign roles to each student, and instruct them to be as historically accurate as possible.

☐ **Readers' Theater**

This center would involve students practicing with a script for a readers' theater presentation and then presenting it to an audience of parents or another class. Students could use the scripts in this book or write their own.

☐ **Discussion Center**

In this center students could discuss the pros and cons of slavery and the activities of the Underground Railroad. Students could use the reading selections and research projects in this book for ideas and information.

☐ **Make a Diorama of the Underground Railroad**

Students at this center could create a 3D model of a slave escape using modeling clay, craft sticks, sand, small fabric pieces, felt, construction paper, and/or small branches. Have students build the models on heavy cardboard or in shoe boxes.

☐ **Clay Figures or Busts**

In this center, students can use modeling clay or inexpensive sculpting clay to make figures or busts of some of the Underground Railroad heroes and heroines they studied. A 25-pound bag of sculpting clay can be sliced into 18 or more pieces with a piece of fish line. Provide craft sticks to carve the features, and have plenty of paper towels available for cleanup.

Annotated Bibliography

Biographies on Harriet Tubman

Carlson, Judy. *Harriet Tubman: Call to Freedom.* Fawcett, 1989. (An excellent treatment of Harriet's life and work for middle graders)

Sterling, Dorothy. *The Story of Harriet Tubman: Freedom Train.* Scholastic, 1954. (A complete, easy-to-read biography of the great conductor)

Diaries

Denenberg, Barry. *When Will This Cruel War Be Over? The Civil War Diary of Emma Simpson.* Dear America Series, Scholastic, 1996. (Well-written diary of a Virginia girl whose life is being destroyed as the Yankees invade her part of the country)

Hansen, Joyce. *I Thought My Soul Would Rise and Fly: The Diary of Patsy, a Freed Girl.* Dear America Series, Scholastic, 1997. (The diary of a black American girl in 1865 who taught herself to read and write and is now experiencing freedom)

McKissack, Patricia C. *A Picture of Freedom: The Diary of Clotee, a Slave Girl.* Dear America Series, Scholastic, 1997. (The diary of a slave who learns to read and write and decides to run to freedom along the Underground Railroad)

Osborne, Mary Pope. *My Brother's Keeper: Virginia's Diary.* My America Series, Scholastic, 2000. (The diary of a Pennsylvania girl at Gettysburg as the battle begins)

Wyeth, Sharon Dennis. *Freedom's Wings: Corey's Diary.* My America Series, Scholastic, 2001. (An easy-to-read story of a slave family escaping from Kentucky)

Fiction

Stowe, Harriet Beecher. *Uncle Tom's Cabin.* Signet, 1981 (reissue). (A classic for middle-grade readers, assign the chapter "Eliza's Escape" to whet their interest.)

Nonfiction

Railroad. Dutton, 1997. (A superb story about these two great leaders)

Bial, Raymond. *The Underground Railroad.* Houghton, Mifflin, 1995. (A brief, pictorial account ofthe Underground Railroad)

Cox, Clinton. *Undying Glory: The Story of the Massachusetts 54th Regiment.* Scholastic, 1991. (Very readable account of the first black regiment in the Civil War)

Freedman, Russell. *Lincoln: A Photobiography.* Scholastic, 1987. (Newbery Award-winning biography of Lincoln for children)

Gorrell, Gena K. *North Star to Freedom: The Story of the Underground Railroad.* Delacorte, 1996. (Interesting vignettes of fugitives and their conductors)

Horton, James Oliver, and Lois Horton. *Slavery and the Making of America.* Oxford University Press, 2005. (An outstanding account of all aspects of American slavery and the efforts of black Americans to escape from it)

Kallen, Stuart A. *Life on the Underground Railroad.* Lucent, 2000. (An excellent middle-grade account of the activities of the Underground Railroad in the context of the nation's history)

Piggins, Carol Ann. *A Multicultural Portrait of the Civil War.* Cavendish, 1994. (The lives and accomplishments of Native Americans, black Americans, and immigrants during the war)

Slave Chronicles

Landau, Elaine. *Slave Narratives: The Journey to Freedom.* (An easy-to-read account of slave life and runaway attempts)

Tackach, James, ed. *Slave Narratives.* Greenhaven, 2001. (Young adult collection of slave stories)

Glossary

abolitionist—a person opposed to slavery

activist—a person who takes action in support of his or her beliefs

agriculture—farming, raising crops and animals

autobiography—the story of a person's life told by himself or herself

biography—the story of a person's life told by someone else

brand—a mark burned on a slave to show ownership

conductor—a person who led fugitive slaves from one safe place to another

Confederate—referring to the states which left the Union

Congress—a group of representatives from different states

contraband—illegal, smuggled goods

depot—a station or hiding place for escaping slaves

emancipate—to give freedom to slaves

federal—relating to the national government, not the states

fugitive—a person on the run from the law

house slave—a slave who worked in an owner's house

liberation—freedom

overseer—a white man paid to keep slaves working and obedient

passengers—fugitive slaves being conducted on the underground railroad

pilot—a person who encouraged slaves to escape

plantation—a large farm usually with one or two cash crops

Quakers—a religious group strongly opposed to slavery

secessionist—one who broke away from the Union and supported the Confederacy

slave hunters—people hired to find runaway slaves

slave—a person who is owned by another person

stationmaster—a person who helped hide escaping slaves

station—a hiding place for escaping slaves

terminal—the final destination for fugitive slaves, usually Canada

Underground Railroad—a system of people and hiding places for helping fugitive slaves

Yankee—a Northerner

Answer Key

Page 21
1. b
2. c
3. a
4. d
5. c
6. d
7. b
8. b
9. a
10. d

Page 22
1. conductors
2. terminals
3. ticket agents
4. train ran off the track
5. smooth trip
6. pilots
7. brakemen
8. stationmasters
9. stations
10. passengers

Page 23
1. b
2. d
3. c
4. d
5. b
6. a
7. c
8. a
9. b
10. a

Page 24
1. a
2. b
3. b
4. d
5. a

6. c
7. c
8. d
9. a
10. b

Page 25
1. b
2. d
3. c
4. b
5. a
6. b
7. c
8. c
9. a
10. d

Page 41
Slave States
1. Alabama
2. Arkansas
3. Delaware
4. Florida
5. Georgia
6. Kentucky
7. Louisiana
8. Maryland
9. Mississippi
10. Missouri
11. North Carolina
12. South Carolina
13. Tennessee
14. Texas
15. Virginia

Free States
1. California
2. Connecticut
3. Illinois
4. Indiana
5. Iowa

6. Kansas
7. Maine
8. Massachusetts
9. Michigan
10. Minnesota
11. New Hampshire
12. New Jersey
13. New York
14. Ohio
15. Oregon
16. Pennsylvania
17. Rhode Island
18. Vermont
19. West Virginia
20. Wisconsin

Page 42
1. Indiana, Ohio, Illinois
2. Pennsylvania
3. New Jersey, Rhode Island
4. Ohio, New York, Maine, Michigan, Vermont, New Hampshire, Minnesota
5. Cuba and the Bahamas